Helen Keller

Women Who Inspire

Terry Barber

Helen Keller is published by
Grass Roots Press, a division of Literacy Services of Canada Ltd.

www.grassrootsbooks.net

ACKNOWLEDGEMENTS

We acknowledge the financial support of the Government of Canada through the Canada Book Fund (CBF) for our publishing activities. Canada

Produced with the assistance of
the Government of Alberta through the
Alberta Multimedia Development Fund. Alberta

Editor: Dr. Pat Campbell
Image research: Dr. Pat Campbell
Book design: Lara Minja

Library and Archives Canada Cataloguing in Publication

Barber, Terry, date
Helen Keller / Terry Barber.

ISBN 978-1-77153-190-0 (paperback)

1. Keller, Helen, 1880-1968. .2. Deafblind women—United States—Biography. 3. Women human rights workers—United States—Biography. 4. Readers for new literates. I. Title.

PE1126.N43B34885 2017 428.6'2 C2016-906602-9

Printed in Canada.

Contents

Helen types her story.

Three Days to See

Helen is 52 years old. Helen loves to read. Helen loves to write. Helen writes books. Helen writes for magazines. Helen writes a story for a magazine. Helen calls the story "Three Days to See."

Helen wants to walk down Fifth Avenue in New York City.

Three Days to See

Helen is blind. In her story, Helen wonders what the world looks like. Helen wants to see, if only for three days. Helen wants to see New York City. Helen wants to see her friends for the first time.

Helen wants to look into her dog's eyes.

Three Days to See

Helen knows her friends are beautiful on the inside. She wants to see the beauty of their faces. Helen loves her dogs, too. Helen wants to see her world. Helen's story shows how sight is a gift.

Helen can feel the beauty of nature.

Three Days to See

Helen is also deaf. In her world, she hears no sound. In her world, she sees no light. Helen lives in a dark and silent world. Most people would find such a life hard to live. Helen turns her life into a gift to the world.

Helen is born in this house.

Early Years

Helen is born in 1880. She is a healthy child. For almost two years, Helen can see and hear. Then Helen becomes sick. The doctor says Helen has brain fever. Helen's eyes hurt. Her eyes feel dry and hot.

Helen is born in Alabama on June 27.

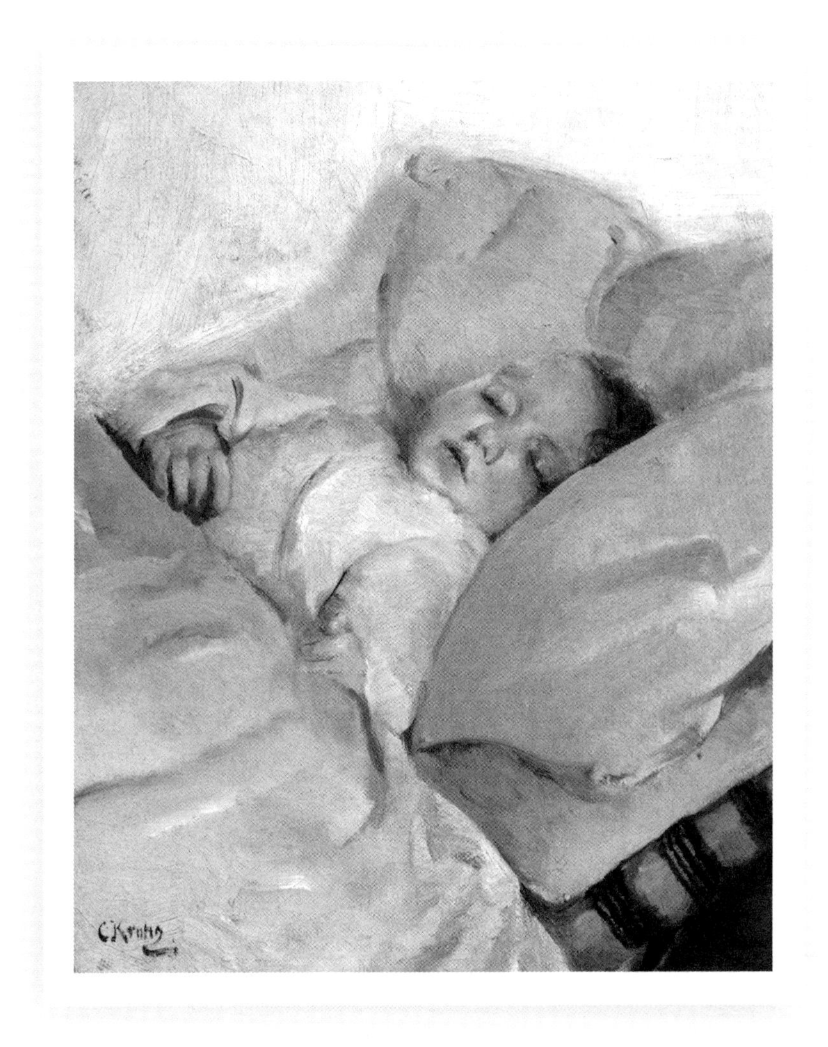

Helen loses sight and hearing
when she is 19 months old.

The doctor thinks Helen will die. She falls into a deep sleep. Her fever passes and she wakes up. The fever leaves Helen deaf and blind. Now, her world is dark and still.

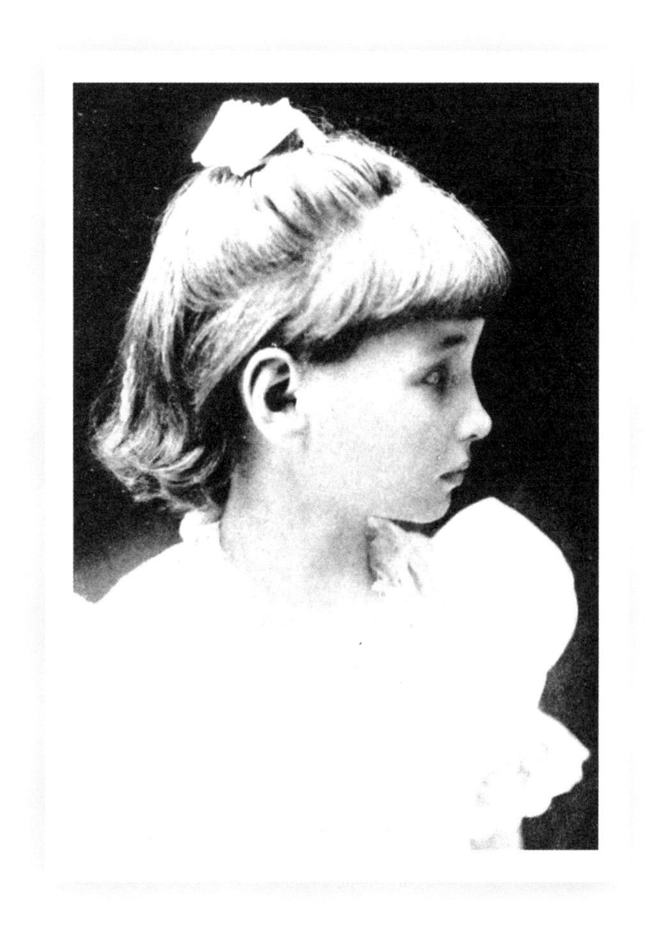

Helen Keller, 1887.

Early Years

If a person is blind, the ears act as windows. If a person is deaf, the eyes help the person hear. Helen faces the world without these senses. Helen is like an **alien** in a strange world.

Helen loves her dog.

Helen's World

No light or sound enters Helen's world. But Helen's world is still rich. She feels her world through touch. Helen can taste her world. Helen's sense of smell is strong. Helen learns her world through these other senses.

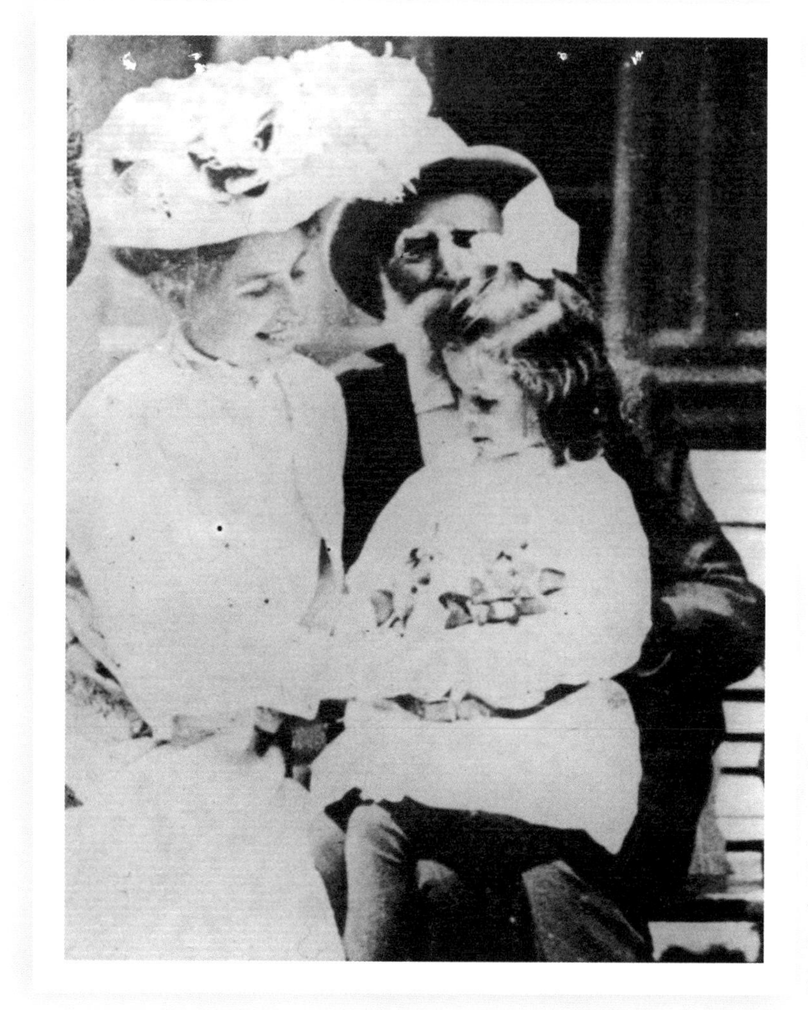

*Identity of adults is not confirmed.

Helen and her parents.

Helen's World

Helen's parents, Kate and Arthur, have little money. Arthur is 20 years older than his wife. But Kate has a strong will. Kate will not give up on Helen. Helen is lucky her mother is strong.

Helen's father is an army **veteran.**

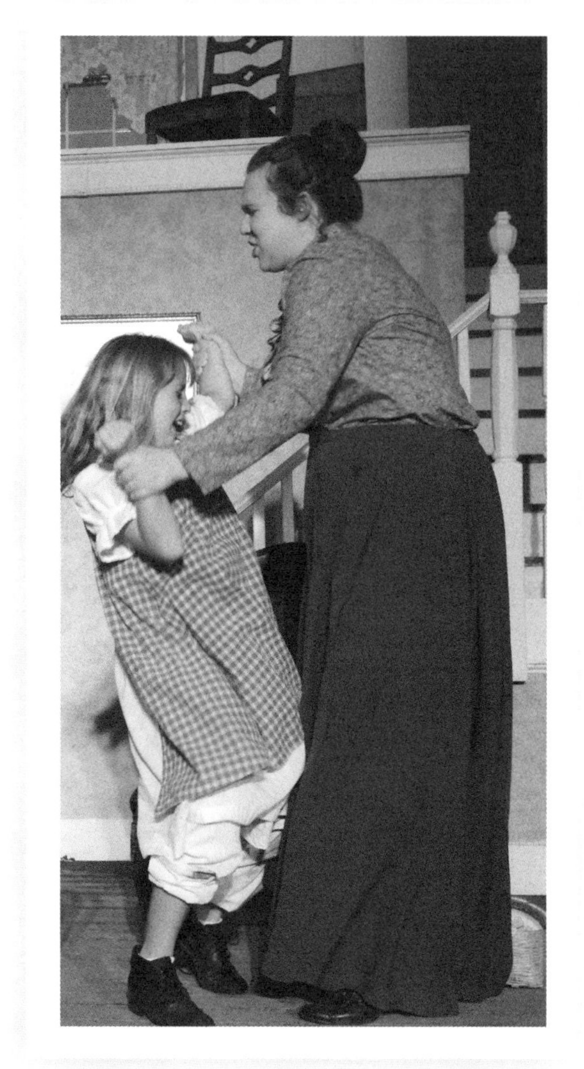

From the play, "The Miracle Worker."

A child has a temper tantrum.

Helen's World

Helen is a bright child. She knows that people speak with each other. Helen wants her world to grow. Helen is mad at the world. Why is she not able to speak or hear or see?

Helen uses 60 hand signs to communicate with her family.

A school for deaf and blind children.

Helen's World

In Helen's time, deaf and blind children are often sent from their homes. People who know Helen call her a monster. Helen has a temper. She kicks people. She bites people. But Kate will not give up on Helen.

Many people with disabilities live in **institutions**.

Helen's teacher is 20 years old.

Helen and Anne

On March 3, 1887, Helen's life changes. A teacher comes into Helen's life. Helen kicks her teacher. Helen punches her teacher. Helen knocks out her teacher's front tooth. The teacher is patient.

Helen's teacher has vision problems.

From The Brewster Historical Society Archives.

Helen and Anne.

Helen and Anne

The teacher's name is Anne Sullivan. Within weeks, Helen trusts Anne. With Anne's help, Helen learns about the bigger world. Anne prints words on Helen's palm. The words spell out the world Helen cannot see or hear.

Helen learns that every object has a name.

Helen uses her fingers to read Braille.

Helen and Anne

Helen's world grows each day she is with Anne. Helen goes to a school for blind children. Helen learns **Braille.** Helen learns to speak, but her speech is never clear. Anne is always by Helen's side, helping her.

Anne finger spells into Helen's hand.

Helen and Anne

Helen goes to college, with Anne by her side. In class, Anne spells every spoken word into Helen's palm. Both women work hard so Helen can get a degree. Helen becomes the first deaf-blind person to get a college degree.

Helen gets her college degree in 1904.

Helen teaches a girl sign language.

Helen's Fame

Helen becomes famous. She uses her fame to improve the lives of others. Helen raises money for deaf and blind people. Helen fights for women's rights. Yet Helen does not have all the rights she deserves.

Helen writes a book called "The Story of My Life."

Helen falls in love.

Helen's Fame

Helen is 36 years old and very beautiful. She works with a reporter named Peter. The couple fall in love. Peter wants to marry Helen. But Helen's family stops the marriage. Helen's family feels she should not marry.

Society feels that people with disabilities should not marry.

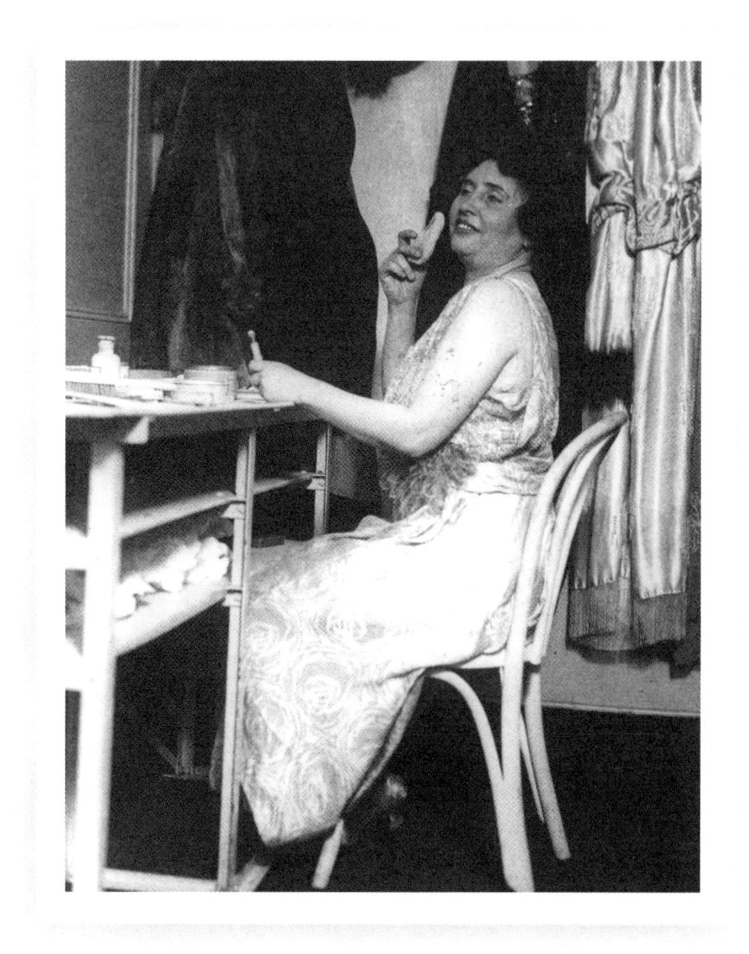

Helen gets ready to go on stage.

Helen's Fame

Later in life, Helen has a **vaudeville** career. Helen loves vaudeville. Helen and Anne answer questions on the stage. "Does Miss Keller think of marriage?" someone asks. "Yes. Are you proposing to me?" Helen answers.

Helen holds Anne's hand.

Helen's Fame

In good times and bad, Anne Sullivan is always there for Helen. They live together for much of Helen's life. Anne dies in 1936. Helen loses her sight and hearing yet again. But Helen, like her mother Kate, is strong.

Anne is Helen's teacher and friend for almost 50 years.

Helen Keller.

Helen's Fame

Helen never forgets Anne. But Helen is able to live without Anne. Life doesn't scare Helen. Old age doesn't scare her. Helen lives until she is 80 years old. As with life, Helen never fears death. Helen dies in peace in 1968.

In 1964, Helen receives the Presidential Medal of Freedom.

Helen Keller sits with her dogs.

Helen's Wisdom

Helen says life's riches "must be felt in the heart." Helen's words open our hearts to the gifts of sight and sound and life.

Glossary

alien: a creature from outer space.

braille: a form of writing. Raised dots represent letters and numbers, which are read by touch.

institution: a place that provides care for people with disabilities.

vaudeville: a stage show that includes comedians, singers, dancers, musicians, animals, etc.

veteran: a person who has served in the military forces.

Talking About the Book

What did you learn about Helen Keller?

What words would you use to describe Helen Keller?

Why is Helen an angry child?

How does Helen's life change?

What challenges does Helen face in her life?

Picture Credits

Front cover (center photo): © Library of Congress, Prints and Photographs Division, LC-DIG-ppmsca-23661; **(small photo)** © Library of Congress, Prints and Photographs Division, LC-USZ62-68305. **Contents page (top left):** © Courtesy of the American Foundation for the Blind, Helen Keller Archive; **(bottom left):** Library of Congress, Prints and Photographs Division, LC-USZ62-78985; **(bottom right):** Library of Congress, Prints and Photographs Division, LC-USZ62-78982. **Page 4:** © Courtesy of Perkins School for the Blind Archives. **Page 6:** © Library of Congress, Prints and Photographs Division, LC-USZ62-48776. **Page 8:** © Library of Congress, Prints and Photographs Division, LC-USZ62-78990. **Page 9:** Library of Congress, Prints and Photographs Division, LC-D420-2963. **Page 10:** © Library of Congress, Prints and Photographs Division, LC-USZ62-101764. **Page 11:** © Library of Congress, Prints and Photographs Division, LC-USZ62-68305 **Page 12:** © Library of Congress, Prints and Photographs Division, HABS ALA-317. **Page 14:** © Bridgeman, Sleeping child, 1862. **Pages 16, 18, 20:** © Courtesy of the American Foundation for the Blind, Helen Keller Archive. **Page 22:** © Library of Congress, Prints and Photographs Division, LC-DIG-highsm-08501. **Page 24:** © Library of Congress, Prints and Photographs Division, LC-G9-Z1-130-726-A. **Page 26:** © Courtesy of the American Foundation for the Blind, Helen Keller Archive. **Page 28:** © From The Brewster Historical Society Archives. **Pages 30, 32:** © Courtesy of the American Foundation for the Blind, Helen Keller Archive. **Page 33:** © Library of Congress, Prints and Photographs Division, LC-USZ62-59957. **Page 34:** © Library of Congress, Prints and Photographs Division, LC-USZ62-78999. **Pages 36, 38:** © Courtesy of the American Foundation for the Blind, Helen Keller Archive. **Page 40:** © Library of Congress, Prints and Photographs Division, H127983. **Page 42:** © Courtesy of Perkins School for the Blind Archives. **Page 44:** © Courtesy of the American Foundation for the Blind, Helen Keller Archive.